LITTLE GRAVEYARDS

poems by
Aleathia Drehmer

ROADSIDE PRESS

Editor: Michele McDannold
Cover Photography: Aleathia Drehmer

Roadside Press
Colchester, Illinois

Table of Contents

To Mary Buth, RN—thank you for always being the voice of reason, a helping hand, a stillness in the chaos. I will forever ask myself in tough situations: "What would Mary Buth do?" I love you, forever.

"Live life when you have it. Life is a splendid gift—there is nothing small about it."
—Florence Nightingale

Angle of Sadness

She came in high with distorted
manifestations of physical pain,
now an ever evolving emotional
quest to find the idea of happiness,
to obtain just a few more pills
to get her through, to ease
the distraction chewing her mind.

Her small children stood at the bedside
like ancient pillars of salt, their long faces
stretched and creased into something old
and stoic beyond their years. Our eyes
flash each others faces, briefly,
and we see ourselves. This truth
is left in the quiet air.

I could tell from experience
and the angle of sadness on their faces,
that they live life by proxy, waiting
for the chance to be free.

By Way of Arkansas

Her face was burnt and peeling
from hours of hot sun on skin
slathered with baby oil.

She talks real tough
with a jaunty fa-get-ah-bout-it attitude.

"Oh yeah," she says, "I'd do it again."
as fingers lightly stroke her wrist
wrapped in pristine gauze.

When she thinks no one is watching,
the truth unfolds, and darkness wraps her
with barbed wings. Tears well over
running thick, black mascara down swollen
cheeks, adding insult to injury.

balancing a cup on the edge of a garbage can

agitated fingers
long and slender
twist the helix of time.

these are two roads
that never cross,
but call his mental state
a bad case of identity theft.

THEY incriminate his coat
as evidence against him.

he refuses to part with it,
lest we discover the truth
locked in the fibers
of the fur trim
he strokes at his neck.

Evidence

Hairs pulled from root
in five different places.

Inside of cheek scraped
with a cardboard blade ten times.

Sterile swab run between tooth
and gum, back and forth five times.

Body inspected for bruises,
scratches, human bites,

pubic hairs plucked and combed
onto white papers.

Secret places that were taken
are cultured for seeds, bringing tears,
and memories best forgotten.

Story replayed by voice (in mind)
                for nurse
                for counselor
                for doctor
                for investigators.

Primes

He slinks around the house,
ginger tail twitching, a seductive finger
to entice from her the golden threads
of her sanity so there are no
more lines to cross.

She catches him in the taunt
with the steel of the knife,
nails digging into his scruff
as a perpendicular line
draws liquid warmth onto her hands.

(2) sets of eyes locked hard,
blistered in emptiness.

Still his tail moves with unseen electricity.
Her volition extracted by the cuts

deep and red, as she finds herself
peeling flesh from bone in ragged strands.

It is (3) here (5) that (7)
the chime (11) of (13)
                              voices
brings (17) up primes,
filtering out words
until they are all that's left.

Rocking
forth and back
rudimentary movements
in rapid succession
                              to the beat
                                        of primes
2, 3, 5,7,11,13
        17

Aleathia Drehmer

"kitty, kitty" she calls
staring at blood soaked
hands in her lap,
linear mind rocking faster
with bits of fur under the nails
and matter congealed to skin.

2, 3, 5,7,11,13   17

Room Two

The snow white afro is blown out,
hairs grow from her chin and
accentuate the blank look
full of lucid lines that change her face in
moments of presence—
the flash of eye, a partial toothed grin.

We dress her like a mannequin, orders bleated
softly four times before her brain
and the periphery take up the translation
and shake hands.

Into the brisk evening, over salted squares
of pavement as pale as her hair,
the wheelchair
rotates.   Halts.

She rises from the seat after several false starts,
shuffles feet in cubic inch increments
until the warm air from the cab
pulls her inward like a soft hug.

Her old black face turns to mine,
alabaster and young with ruby cheeks,
and the curl of her lip turns up in a smile:

"Honey, where is my purse?" she says.

and I watch how easily
her face falls back
into nothingness.

My laughter rises into the night,
her daughter's lilt a half pitch above mine,
as our notes mix and float into this time
of sick parents, and final holidays,

emblazoning moments like these into cells
for when there are no more left to make.

Saints in Waiting

At midnight, an old man hovers
in the waiting area, his small, blue eyes
muddied from years of alcohol and smoke.

I ask if I can help him and he opens his mouth,
teeth rotting, breath laced with drink,
and tells me he needs to talk.

He starts with his worries (no one loves me)
while nervously touching his face.
There is sickness in his family,
wrongs and rights committed unto others,
love and sadness, old war times,
and how the wife always tells him to
SHUT UP   (you bastard)

Loving words spill from him
about his dead father, a man always

on the straight and narrow, a man
who spoke line after line from the Bible
in a stern tone.

He speaks of his two sisters
both smart and good looking,
accomplished teachers and nurses,
                    his insignificance apparent,
and of their distance (with)in
geographical closeness.

Plastic covered pictures in his wallet
are flipped, neat faces of children
and grandchildren he never sees,
or holds, run by in animation.

He tells me of the time his son
hugged him for no reason,
tears welling in his eyes, rims red and moist
as he carefully touches them   away

(can't waste what little I have)

I stand there with shades of (in)difference,
thinking of stories about old beggars
at the roadside whom no one will help
with signs pleading:

> *Will work for food*

Prophets, deities, monks, saints in waiting,
test the fiber of humanity, test my soul's
moral fortitude as I lay my hand
on his arm and smile.

Pink Basin

I watched as the doctor
pulled from her body
the remains
of her unborn child,
watched as it
traveled through the air
clamped tightly
in small, steel forceps,
the distance like a mile
until it reached
my pink, kidney shaped
emesis basin.

I looked up at her
as he tapped the forceps
on the side of the plastic,
and we shared
a piece of soul

at that moment,
she saw in my face
that the hope
of tiny fingers
and tiny toes
lay in my hands,
gently curved.

Black Seas

Regression happens with age,
bodies morph into sharp, geometric
renditions of flesh with insipid harsh angles.

Her face engulfed by the caverns
her sockets make, muddied pools
empty and still with no flickering fire
cast about the walls.

The skin stretched over her face looks waxy
and I beckon the notion
to call Madame Tussaud,
but this woman lacks singular
importance in the world,
one old leaf ready to be blown about
and put back to the earth.
No accolades for her bravery.

I sit here in the dark watching her breath hover,
the vapor shaped in the image of Gabriel,
and I let the room fall away from me.

Her collarbone creates a valley that could hold
the Black Sea, her mind lost somewhere
between youth and release, and I want to touch
the sweat collecting there.
Her salted life seeping up from her center
as if a spring of groundwater.

My fingers reach out silently
as she opens her eyes in one, small moment
of lucidity to ask me,

"Am I still alive?"

Her face alight in that second showing me
the heartbreak of lovers, meals cooked,

children swaddled, and presents
given with knowing.

"Yes," I tell her. "Yes."

False Dreams of a Nightingale

People move in and out
of the tables around us,
each ordering plates of eggs and toast.
The smell of pancakes with maple syrup
is sickly sweet after long hours in the ER,
                                    saving lives.

Both of us sit here in an abbreviated
second wind, the years showing on her face
as I am sure they also do on mine,
with all the losses we cannot forget.

There are tears over shared tragedies,
still fresh and painful,
that lead to ragged napkins
crumpled on the table amongst
the empty creamers and cold coffee.

She leaves the spot across from me
and I am suddenly aware of what this life
will become; one thankless night after another,
spanned over the decades of my life, until I am
                                          here again

watching people drip eggs on their shirts.
We make straws into geometric designs
in the awkward silences between bites
and I think to myself
that I should have hugged her
when she told me her friend died.

By the tail

She is the definition
of a situation gone wrong—
her body filled with sleeping pills,
Morphine, and Motrin,
enough to stop organs in their tracks;
arms laden with horse on a late night death ride
into the blackest sky she'd ever seen.

Thirty minutes down,
rocking in the arms of Grim,
kissed by his poisonous tongue when she sees
the pin-prick lights cascading
into fluorescent floods.

Faces around her bleed awe
at what they have returned,
an unwilling body and a brain
left to a fate worse than death,
worse than the life she was trying to leave.

Time steals sinew and fat until she is little more
than the living dead with pinched blue eyes
perpetually angry and frightened,
teeth gnashing involuntarily,
limbs contracted like bird wings.

She is alive in a wasting body,
a prisoner of her own design,
and I want to take her picture
to show my daughter what happens
when the devil has you by the tail,
when you think you are invincible,
only to realize there is no such thing.
There is only luck, and luck run dry.

Easy Medicine

Skin heals from the inside out.
We watch the wounds close,
pushing up new cells daily.

It's her own small miracle
self-created again and again
            again and again
with the razor slowly biting
into microcosmic layers.

Each thickness has its own dimension in time
and she stands witness to blood rising
from skin folds, valleys made
from her innate need for destruction.

A river is nourished with every ripple
it pushes up over the banks, spilling
into the empty valley of her heart.

It's easy medicine.

Each groove alleviating pain quicker
than any pill or couch session.
It makes her remember, that despite it all,
she's still alive.

Electra

She has tattooed
the names
of all her lovers
on various
lines of her body,
the most important
conquests
highly visible,
banners of her victory,
no secrets to be kept.

It settles over me
strangely and deeply
that the tender spot
of her neck
below the ear,
the coveted place
a lover might stop

to steal a kiss
as he traverses
his way to bigger
and better things
is inked crisply
with the letters
of her father's name.

Vera

She talks to God
about not wanting
to turn eighty-three.
She is at peace
with this life she has lived,
having been through
enough birthdays,
anniversaries,
and Easters
to feel like she has not
missed anything.

There is a child-like
sweetness about her face,
with its wrinkles,
and soft edges around
the curve of her mouth.
There still lives

a mischievous twinkle
in the squint of her blue eyes.

The space around her
speaks of years of joy,
sadness,
peace,
and the belonging
to something greater
than I might ever know.
It speaks of great loves lost,
and a long, life
well lived.

She leans into me,
our shoulders touching gently
as I sit on her hospital bed,
and tells me with soft voice
and ease of mind,
that she has asked God

for a long nap.

Tectonics

When he cries
the soft bones
of his skull,
not yet connected,
shift and heave
in human
plate tectonics.
His ocean of skin,
waves of fine hair,
and tiny fingers
clutching at my hand
like a seabird
fishing the surface
of choppy waters
not knowing he has been
carried out to sea.

Fate is a Cruel Notion

We call him "boy"
as his one hour on the outside
of safety has not afforded
him more than that.

His face sweet with tell-tale puckered lips,
toes and fingers accounted for
more than once, but his skin
the color of fresh bruises or violet dawn—
how the shadowed Monkshood
in spring dusk learns to be tragic.

We swarm above him like bees,
the nectar of life obsessive
in our praying hearts;
our heads culling every knowledge bestowed,
while hands love and work on him as one.

His body gives no struggle,
no labor for breath, no cry for mercy—
only random flexes from tiny legs.

The world around me ceases.
No noise, no hearts beating,
and all rational thought,
laced with code of conduct,
bereft in the room as I kiss
his smooth heel and made a wish.

Curled

She is 98 going on 50
and I am changing her back
into her clothes for discharge home.

We chat about remembering
not to take too many of her new pills
without talking to the doctor,
as she rests a hand upon my forearm,
her touch light and feathery
with fragile, thin skin.

I look into her eyes to find
the edges reddening, brim with sad tears
on the brink of spilling.

She tells me she doesn't understand
why sickness has found her family
so late in her life.

She grips me now with tiny fingers,
speaking of her son curled
in a bed from stroke,
how he had never hurt anyone in his life
to deserve such an end,
such a fate.

There is nothing I can say
so I start to cry, place my hand
upon her brittle, gray hair

sliding it down until it rests
on her cheek to catch the tear
that got away.

The Quickness

I can't seem
to get used to the sound,
the feeling
of ribs cracking
under the pressure of my hands,
and the solemn idea
that the force of my body
that I put forth to heal,
can cut to the quick
and destroy as easily
as it can save.

iPod

Inside your brain
lives a tumor
that is crushing half
of the butterfly
nestled in your white matter.

The doctor was telling you
this as I located your son
in the waiting area.
He sat there alone,
back hunched over
with arms resting
on his knees.

Familiar white strings
dangled from his ears,
and I saw the iPod
cradled in his hands,

toes tapping to a beat
only he could hear.

He tugged the strings
from his ears as he saw me
come near him,
questions written across
his innocent forehead
about the condition
of his dad.

He followed me
to the darkened room,
and all I could bring
myself to think about
is the last song he
listened to before he
found out his father
would soon die.

Women's Liberation

S(he) is working her way
towards being a woman—
face done thick with pancake make-up,
hair pulled tight and close to the head.

S(he) is going for a down stated look,
something All-American
decked out in Juicy sweats
and a fitted women's t-shirt.

S(he) sits in my low-slug chair,
legs crossed lady-like with hands
resting Victorian on knee; her
fingernails long and filed and polished.

Art Can't Save Me Now

There is an urgency around her neck
his finger's watermark left indelible
from now on, changing color, solidifying
and taunting memories

      from me
      from left hooks to my jaw
      from tire marks on my mother's bones
      from babysitter's unrecognizable face.

I want to shake her but he has
done a fair job of that
though not enough to make her leave

even when I tell her love doesn't look like this,
doesn't raise hands, doesn't steal
your breath by force, doesn't threaten
icy river graves out of jealousy,

she can't look me in the eye when she says
she feels sorry for people who have no one,
even those who beg her to come back
no matter the cost.

Estimated Losses

On the brink of death,
laden with possibilities,
name—life—something
coveted and created,
always chasing after
10 fingers
10 toes
1 smile
at
any cost.

She looks at me, her face ashen with a worry
that only comes on the coattails of a dying life,
and tells me she doesn't feel so well.

I try to hide my knowledge from her, the knowing
that her belly is rising with blood and the faded
dreams of motherhood. It dangles by a thread.

My hand touches hers understanding
the chances we'll take
for sweet replications
of our love.

Beyond Recognition

He looks at her crying face
marked sharply with fear
as he asks himself
Who is this woman?

He's made her suffer—
fingers gripped into
the bones of her arm
imprinting this new filth,
erasing forty years
in a series of strikes:

blow by blow
there is emptiness,
a Zen-less inhumanity
seizing every wire
in his brain.

Her tears suddenly reach him,
softening his face, slackening his body
while he wonders why his wife is crying,
bruised and beaten, and looks at his hands,
these masterful weapons of flesh.

He has nothing left
but a face
he can't recognize.

Self-made Eggs

She is a quarantined animal in her own house,
toes lightly treading over broken shells
of her self-made eggs.

She is the whisper you don't hear
recycling her breath—
part woman, part willow.

She is the rabbit frozen mid-movement
in new grass, heart racing
and senses on fire.

She is wrists bound with invisible ropes of fear
skin chaffed and red— bleeding
words she has no bravery to speak.

Tweaked

He shambles up to you as if I were invisible—
skin black and tight, pupils blown inside
the whites of his eyes.

Brother can you spare some change for food?

His body an aggressive shell, hand stretched out
inches from your chest
and closer than either of us
like as I patted my front pocket
filled with crisp twenty dollar bills.

My hand drops as you filch
a few bucks from your jeans
and put it into that empty-handed soul.

As he turns to go you speak
over the din of traffic....*spend it on food man.*

We both know
      that
will never happen.

Exit 48
For Marlene

When I came here before
it was for fractured solitude,
trucks and cars busily moving on the highway,
my mind was so full of questions
it seemed empty.

Now, the crickets chirp
a maddening scream for rain
and the golden rod is still green and waiting,
hoping for the sun to keep its post.
The hills hide in a haze of humidity
that is unbearable to this body.

I come here now to mourn
before and after work—

to put questions into the field
knowing there will be no answers,
ever, to what my soul needs to hear.

Now, I stand at the weeping willow
with its empty summer branches
wondering if I'll lose another great woman
in my life, a friend who knows
all my secrets and keeps them.

I can't mourn, not yet,
but my heart has a heaviness
that is burdened over and over again.
The wheel of life spins
with so many leaving, so few getting on.

I look to the dried thistle for strength—prickly
and seemingly dead, but still standing,
still fighting, still knowing it has to spread
its seeds of wisdom for another day.

Silent Movies

The scariest thing about cancer
is my own body fighting against me
with cells stuttering and stacking
like a deep hidden obsession
I never learned to let go of.

The crater cut into the side of my face—
a bullet hole, an excavation,
an empty mineshaft,
filled with questions no one but the universe
has the answers for. It's a dark ugliness
I show myself like an outdoor silent movie.

There is pain in places I've never imagined,
my smile tugging on the edges
of the star-shaped, pursed rim of flesh
shrunken half its size by the pull
of an invisible string for vanity
in the guise of healing.

But the thing that hurts the most
is the pale face of my child, the light sweat
collecting on their brow, the clutching
of their stomach as the reality of cancer
finally sets in. It's a fear
I can't find the words to allay.

Our Labored Breaths
For Lisa

No one understands my trauma
like you do, the way it carves
an immeasurable piece of flesh
from places well hidden.
It is the perfect murderer, charming
and quick.

The silence in our friendship
speaks volumes to the fact
we know how little fixing
each other fills us. It's the
need to exist in the company
of another.

This is the true art of letting go
from the years of abuse
disguised as self-sabotage.

It is the walk in the woods,
our labored breaths mixing
with pine and the sound of creeks
run dry.

Dress Rehearsal

The room is shrouded in darkness,
a heavy rattle from the man's chest
fills the room with a nurse's knowing,
Death makes its voice heard.

His two daughters sit legs akimbo
in the pale light that seeps through
the blinds; one watches his chest
rise and fall, the other the Morphine
dripping into his veins.   Both waiting.

Each time I return to the room,
their bodies are in different positions
staring into the hazy afternoon searching
for an ending that just won't come.

The Slow Dance

He tells me a story about his wife
and their favorite song, how over
the years of marriage they're still in love.
Under my mask, I smile at the idea.

*Whenever it comes on the radio
we always slow dance,* he tells me.
A soft look of remembering
flutters across his face.

*One time while driving to Georgia,
in the middle of the night, "Unchained Melody"
came on the radio. The kids were asleep
in the back seat and we pulled over
to the side of the highway
and danced in front of the headlights.*

I stayed busy in his hospital room to keep
from letting the tears spill over thinking
about how we could all spend a lifetime
looking for a love so sweet.

Aleathia Drehmer is the creator and editor of *Durable Goods: The Missouri Collective* which featured poetry from high school students affected by trauma. She was once the editor of *In Between Altered States,* co-editor of *Full of Crow* and *Zygote in My Coffee,* and art editor of *Regardless of Authority.* Aleathia is the author of seven chapbooks and currently has three collections of poetry available: *We Don't Get to Write the Ending* (Roadside Press), *Looking for Wild Things* (Impspired), and *Layers of Half-Sung Hymns* (Cajun Mutt Press). She hosts open mic poetry readings at Card Carrying Books and Gifts in Corning, NY and had a Poetry in Play feature in May 2023 with the ARTS Council of the Southern Finger Lakes. You can follow Aleathia's journey at www.aleathiadrehmer.com

MORE ROADSIDE PRESS TITLES

MORE ROADSIDE PRESS TITLES